PROFESSIONAL ETHICS

PROFESSIONAL ETHICS

DR TAMANA BAHLOL

Contents

Acknowledgements

- Among any society's most important institutions are the social structures by which the society controls the use of specialized knowledge and skills. This is particularly true when highly valued aspects of human life depend on such expertise, and all the more so if acquiring such expertise requires lengthy theoretical education and intensive training in its practical application under the supervision of those already expert, thus rendering the knowledge and skill in its application unavoidably exclusive.
- Professional ethics are principles that govern the behaviour of a person or group in a business environment. Like values, professional ethics provide rules on how a person should act towards other people and institutions in such an environment.

CHAPTER ONE

- Social control over the use of such knowledge and skills is important because the members of the expert group could use their exclusive expertise solely for their own benefit or even hold society hostage to their expertise. But those who might exert such control, if they are outside the expert group, cannot depend on their understanding of this expertise precisely because they lack the relevant knowledge and practical training. How, then, can a society control the use of important, specialized expertise and render those outside the expert group secure so that they will be able to enjoy the values that depend on it? One of the most important social structures developed to this end is the institution of profession.
- In many people's minds, it is by publicly taking an oath that a person becomes a professional and acquires specifically professional obligations; and indeed the term profession does come to us from the Latin professio that comes in turn from the Greek verb prophaino, "to declare publicly." But it is not the oath that classically concludes professional training that creates professionals or produces their special obligations. It is in their presenting themselves

- The oath that many new professionals take is rather a reminder to those beginning professional practice that important ethical commitments go with it and a public assurance to the larger community by the new practitioners that they understand and accept this reality.

  In the minds of many mature professionals, it was not the formal oath nor any other public activity that made them professionals, but rather their personal sense of vocation, of a calling or of being called, to this way of life. There is something truly admirable in this view of profession because professional practice is ethically challenging enough that only those with a deep sense of personal ethical commitment will manage its challenges well. But it would be a serious mistake to put all the focus on the person of the committed professional and none on the important social systems in which such a person functions.

- to others as possessors and practitioners of a profession's expertise that they declare publicly that they are members of a profession and accept its ethical commitments as their own.

- Professional ethics are standards set by professional organizations for the behavior and values of people working within a specific field. Codes of professional ethics are established in order to provide guidance to professionals, usually to not abuse client relationships and preserve the integrity and reputation of the applicable profession. When a person violates one or more of these promulgated ethics, he or she is subject to disciplinary action by the governing body of the profession. A high level of adherence to a code of professional ethics is needed so that the public will be confident in the moral standards of those working in the field. Codes of professional ethics are commonly applied to professionals in the fields of accounting, law, and medicine.

- First, the content of the ethic of each profession—that is, the ethic that the committed professional is called to practice—is the content of an ongoing dialogue between the profession as a whole and the larger community within which it practices. Second, every professional's practice is necessarily practice in conjunction with someone served, frequently a capable, independent decision maker and always someone whose well-being is not fully defined by the values of the profession. The vocation or calling of the committed professional is precisely a social vocation, a calling to ethical relationships with those served in the context of the whole profession's proper relationship to the larger community.

- The practice of specialized expertise and the special moral commitments associated with professional practice are what most differentiate a profession from other occupations. All the ways in which people spend their time earning a living involve skills and knowledge of value to others and involve relationships with others that have ethical significance, at a minimum the prohibition of coercion and the requirement that people honor their contracts that characterizes marketplace relationships. But the analysis just offered indicates that specifically professional practice involves a particular combination of institutionalized expertise and special ethical obligations over and above the obligations of the marketplace. It is these characteristics taken together that differentiate professions from other occupation.

- Moreover, for the same reason, only persons fully educated in both knowledge and practice of a profession's expertise can be relied on to judge correctly the need for expert intervention in a given situation or to judge the quality of such an intervention as it is being carried out. Such judgments by those not so trained are not dependable. Because of the importance of what is at stake, it is not sufficient to judge the performance solely on the basis of its long-term outcomes, even when the nonexpert can accomplish such a judgment unaided. Long-term outcomes will not be known for some time, and the risk of negative consequences in the meantime, in a matter of great importance, is too great.

- THE RELATIONSHIP BETWEEN THE PROFESSION AND THE LARGER COMMUNITY. The activities of every profession also involve diverse relationships between the profession as a group, or its individual members, and persons who are neither co-professionals nor clients. These relationships may involve the larger community as a whole, various significant subgroups, or specific individuals. Every profession, precisely because it is permitted to be self-regulating, for example, owes the larger community the effort needed to carry out this task conscientiously. This includes providing and monitoring educational programs and institutions in which new members of the profession receive their formation as professionals; monitoring the collective activities of members of the profession in their various professional organizations to make sure that these organizations act in ways consistent with the other professional obligations of the members; and having measures in place to monitor and correct incompetent or other professionally inappropriate practice on the part of individual members of the group.

Each profession has an educational obligation to the larger community. The reason is that both through actions of its individual members and through collective actions, every profession functions as the principal educator of the community regarding those elements of the profession's expertise that the lay community needs to understand in order to function effectively in ordinary life. Thus, for example, the health professions have obligations regarding public education in matters of ordinary health self-care and hygiene; and the engineering and scientific professions have obligations to educate regarding safety practices that the lay community needs to know in daily life.

A more subtle kind of obligation in relation to the larger community has to do with the content of key value concepts that become part of the public culture and play crucial roles in people's private lives and especially in public policy, but whose content is significantly influenced by the members of a profession or of a group of professions. For example, the engineering professions have a powerful formative influence on the culturally dominant notions of safety and physical risk; the health professions are more responsible than any other group for educating the public about what it means to be healthy; and so on. This is an area of professional obligation to the larger community that has received little attention but is of continuing ethical significance.

ACCESS TO PROFESSIONAL SERVICES. Professional services are distributed within a society by a complex system of economic, legal, and social structures. These structures principally determine who in the society will have access to the services of the professions when they need them. But because every professional is committed to the values that are central to his profession, no professional can consistently be indifferent when a significant number of people in the society need professional assistance to achieve these values and their need remains unmet.

There is, however, no single best answer to the question, "What ought I do when the society's distribution system leaves people in need of my profession's services without access to them?" Individual professionals will respond to this aspect of their professional obligation in different ways. For some it will involve pro bono or charity service of one sort or another. For others it will involve advocacy for changes in the distribution system or for publicly funded programs to provide services for the underserved. Others may focus on the value judgments being made by public decision makers who are arguably giving too low a priority to the kinds of well-being the profession provides. But in any case, access to the profession's services on the part of those in the society who need them is a matter that deserves special notice and explicit attention in the articulation of every profession's ethic.

INTEGRITY AND EDUCATION. Finally, there is that very subtle component of conduct by which a person communicates to others what she stands for, not only in the person's acts themselves but also in how these acts are chosen and in how the person presents herself to others in carrying them out. The two words that seem to communicate the core of this concern are integrity and education, especially when the two words are paired.

Each profession stands for, or "professes," certain values that it is committed to bringing about both for its clients individually and for the community at large. But a professional's personal priorities may communicate a different set of values, even though the professional's choices of interventions for clients and his efforts to secure appropriate relationships with clients all conform to accepted standards. Concern with this kind of communication to their patients and to the general public, for example, motivates some health professionals to establish in their personal lives patterns of healthy living consonant with what they say to their patients. Failure to attend to this element of professional commitment also makes illegal personal activities on the part of lawyers somehow doubly wrong.

Professionals may be obligated, then, to do some things and to refrain from doing others in order to remain true to the values that their profession stands for and thereby to educate others in these values by their own example.

There are undoubtedly other useful ways of dividing the general topic of professional obligation besides these nine categories. The point is that conceptual tools such as the key features of the institution of profession and the principal categories of professional obligation can assist professionals in determining their own obligations in general and in particular cases, and can assist scholars and educators of professional ethics to gain a clearer understanding of professional practice and of the ethical standards that apply to it.

Alternative Views of Profession

The account just given explains the institution of profession in terms of its function in society, as a means by which a society secures the benefits of specialized expertise for its members and prevents or at least limits its misuse by those who possess it. Like every account of a thing's function, this account is both descriptive and normative. It describes how professions and their members act, at least for the most part, and it identifies sets of standards by which their successes and failures to act in those ways are to be judged.

The principal alternative ways of explaining the institution of profession can be described under four headings: historical, critical functionalist, radical democratic, and personalist. Each of these approaches separates the descriptive and normative elements that are interwoven in a functionalist account, with the first and second stressing the descriptive elements and the third and fourth the normative elements.

Historical explanations of the institution of profession identify, through historical study, a developmental pattern that brings an occupational group to the point of being considered a profession. This pattern is then used normatively to determine whether particular occupational groups qualify as professions and what patterns of conduct by these groups conform or do not conform to the pattern. Some historical studies of professions do not purport to explain the institution of profession, of course, but simply tell part of its story without attempting to draw normative conclusions. Historical explanations may depend, at least initially, on some functionalist account of profession or on the selection of certain occupations, in their contemporary form or otherwise, as endpoints or at least markers of the developmental process being studied. But once a developmental explanation has been formulated, it can then be offered to replace functionalist accounts on the grounds that these are excessively idealized and are not adequately descriptive of the current or historical conduct of relevant groups. For example, the medical profession in the mid-twentieth century has been described as the product of a process of monopolization, or gradual acquisition of control by an exclusive group over a segment of market activity over the years (Berlant). The institution of profession generally has been described as a specialized mechanism for maintaining economic power and class-based status and dominance (Larson).

Some critics of the professions formulate a functionalist account of the institution for themselves, or accept someone else's, and then use its normative content to critique current patterns of conduct of individuals and organizations within a particular profession or across the professions generally (Freidson). Other functionalist critics argue that currently accepted functionalist accounts are so idealized—that is, pay so little attention to the gap between what is described as the profession's function and the profession's actual conduct—that they leave unchallenged actual or potential harm to the community by the professions or at least do not call upon the professions strongly enough to correct their inadequacies for the community's sake. Therefore, an alternative account of the function of professions and professionals is proposed, and its implications for professional conduct are identified (Kultgen).

Radical democratic critics of the institution of profession believe that any society that accepts this institution makes a profound mistake. It is central to the institution of profession that the possession of expertise is a basis of power and that one element of that power is a grant of autonomy to those possessed of it. By institutionalizing deep inequalities of power and autonomy in this way, these critics argue, a society makes the achievement of genuine democracy almost impossible. According to the radical democrat, the failures in conduct pointed out by functionalist critics and the developmental patterns leading to monopoly and to other forms of economic and class-based inequality that the historical critics point out are not historically contingent events but the inevitable outcomes of the inherently undemocratic constitution of the institution of profession. For these thinkers the solution, on which the well-being of the human community depends, is to do away with the institution of profession and all other institutions grounded on undemocratic premises (Illich, 1973, 1976).

The personalist explanation of profession identifies the individual professional's act of personal commitment upon entering a profession as the basis of everything morally significant about the institution of profession. As centuries ago a solemn vow initiated a person's membership into a profession—a vestige of which remains, for example, in the ceremony in which new physicians speak the Hippocratic Oath—so today the act of personal commitment by each member of a profession is what brings the profession continually into being and gives it its character. The contents of a profession's norms are determined by the contents of these personal acts of commitment; and the professional who falls short in conduct fails above all to honor her own commitment to serve others, rather than failing to follow a norm created and sustained principally, according to the account proposed here, by the mutual effort of the profession and the community at large (Pellegrino; Pellegrino and Thomasma).

Each of these approaches stresses a feature of the institution of profession that standard functionalist accounts are held to overlook or underestimate: the developmental patterns by which professions and professionals are formed; the extent to which professions' and professionals' actual conduct falls short of the functionalist's proposed norms; the undemocratic character of exclusive expertise; and the centrality of the act of commitment by which a person becomes a professional. More complex functionalist accounts could incorporate much that is stressed in these other approaches, as more complex versions of each of them could incorporate emphases and concerns from the others. From the point of view of understanding professions as they exist, in other words, each of these approaches teaches something of importance and all deserve careful study.

Changing Times, Changing Standards, Changing Concepts

It is not only the conduct of individuals and groups, as measured by professional norms, that can fall short of what ought to be. Professional norms themselves can fall short of what they ought to be, particularly when important characteristics of a society undergo change. There was a time, for example, when the general level of education in the United States may well have justified an ethics in which the ideal patient–practitioner relationship for physicians and dentists conformed to the guild model rather than the interactive model, whereas the latter has become normative for these professions in the years since the 1970s.

A profession's norms and the institution of profession itself are human constructs and, like all things of human making, they can fall short of their intended goals, and the goals themselves can change with changing times. When norms and institutions are no longer able to do the tasks that a society needs them to do, then the society is justified in trying to change them. But social structures such as professions are inherently conservative, in the root sense of that word; they exist to preserve a mode of acting or of organizing conduct that has proven fruitful, and they preserve it by forming in their participants strong habits of perceiving, judging, and acting in ways that support it.

So when times and expectations change, or people's values or abilities change, or the surrounding social institutions change, then it is important to reexamine the relevant norms and institutions to see if they are still appropriate and to change them if they are not, even if this involves a major transformation of a particular profession's norms across many of the nine categories. One of the weaknesses of functionalist accounts of the institution of profession in the minds of critics is that such accounts seem to say that whatever is the case is what ought to be the case. But, like the other four approaches, the functionalist account is simply a conceptual tool whose purpose is to help a society understand what it has when it has a particular profession with a particular set of norms so that the society can then make a judgment on whether that is the profession that ought to exist.

In an analogous way, the new professional enters a profession whose norms are already in place. This does not mean that these norms cannot be changed, but they achieve their content by means of an ongoing dialogue between the profession and the larger community, and they change their content in the same way. So the new professional cannot create the contents of his professional obligations out of whole cloth. Yet, even in the individual case, the norms of the profession are not the ultimate determiners of right and wrong. If these norms are in conflict with one another or with other important moral considerations, or if they are severely defective in some way, then the professional must form his own conscience to decide how to act. Situations arise in which conscientious disobedience of a professional norm is what a person's moral judgment requires when all things about a situation are considered.

By what standards should a society judge a profession's norms when their adequacy to the society's needs is in question? By what standard should the institution of profession itself be judged? By what standard should the individual professional form her own conscience when conflict or severe doubt about the adequacy of a professional norm in a particular case suggests that conscientious disobedience may be the correct path? Surely not by the norms of the profession, because these are precisely what are being challenged when such questions arise. It is to the deeper values and standards of human conduct and social life that individuals must turn at such times, for it is upon them that the norms of professions rest for their moral force in the first place.

As is true for many other human institutions, if the institution of profession did not exist, it or something like it would need to be invented in order for people to live together effectively. For no one person can master all the knowledge and skills on which the achievement of so many important values in human life depend. But, like other human institutions, the institution of profession as a whole, and each individual profession, and each normative feature of each profession, requires regular ethical scrutiny to make sure it continues to fulfill the purposes for which it was made. One of the principal roles of the field of bioethics and its practitioners is to provide the members of the health professions and the larger community with effective conceptual tools to employ in this scrutiny.

- Ethical principles

Ethical principles underpin all professional codes of conduct. Ethical principles may differ depending on the profession; for example, professional ethics that relate to medical practitioners will differ from those that relate to lawyers or real estate agents.

However, there are some universal ethical principles that apply across all professions, including:

honesty

trustworthiness

loyalty

respect for others

adherence to the law

doing good and avoiding harm to others

accountability.

Codes of conduct

Professional codes of conduct draw on these professional ethical principles as the basis for prescribing required standards of behaviour for members of a profession. They also seek to set out the expectations that the profession and society have of its members.

The intention of codes of conduct is to provide guidelines for the minimum standard of appropriate behaviour in a professional context. Codes of conduct sit alongside the general law of the land and the personal values of members of the profession.

- rofessional codes of conduct provide benefits to:

    the public, as they build confidence in the profession's trustworthiness

    clients, as they provide greater transparency and certainty about how their affairs will be handled

    members of the profession, as they provide a supporting framework for resisting pressure to act inappropriately, and for making acceptable decisions in what may be 'grey areas'

    the profession as a whole, as they provide a common understanding of acceptable practice which builds collegiality and allows for fairer disciplinary procedures

    others dealing with the profession, as the profession will be seen as more reliable and easier to deal with.

- Other contributors to professional ethics

    Fiduciary duties

    When an adviser agrees to assist a client, they agree to take on a level of responsibility for that person and their immigration matter. The client becomes dependent on the adviser in relation to that assistance. This is a fiduciary relationship between the fiduciary (the adviser) and a principal (the client). Even without a Code this fiduciary relationship means the adviser has certain obligations to their client.

Contractual obligations

When an adviser enters into a contract (or written agreement) with a client this creates legally binding obligations to perform the terms of the contract in a particular way. This includes a duty to act with diligence, due care and skill, and also implies obligations such as confidentiality and honesty, even if they are not specifically set out in the contract.

Many ethical issues are likely to stem from advisers' relationships with clients. Most of these can be overcome by having clear terms in a written agreement about how certain matters will be dealt with, such as the sharing of confidential information, the use of interpreters, refunds and invoicing. More information on written agreements can be found in the Code of Conduct Toolkit.

- Most professionals have internally enforced codes of practice that members of the profession must follow to prevent exploitation of the client and to preserve the integrity and reputation of the profession. This is not only for the benefit of the client but also for the benefit of those belonging to that profession. Disciplinary codes allow the profession to define a standard of conduct and ensure that individual practitioners meet this standard, by disciplining them from the professional body if they do not practice accordingly. This allows those professionals who act with a conscience to practice in the knowledge that they will not be undermined commercially by those who have fewer ethical qualms. It also maintains the public's trust in the profession, encouraging the public to continue seeking their services.
- Internal regulation

In cases where professional bodies regulate their own ethics, there are possibilities for such bodies to become self-serving and fail to follow their own ethical code when dealing with renegade members. This is particularly true of professions in which they have almost a complete monopoly on a particular area of knowledge. For example, until recently, the English courts deferred to the professional consensus on matters relating to their practice that lay outside case law and legislation

- Statutory regulation

  In many countries there is some statutory regulation of professional ethical standards such as the statutory bodies that regulate nursing and midwifery in England and Wales.Failure to comply with these standards can thus become a matter for the courts.

- Examples

  For example, a lay member of the public should not be held responsible for failing to act to save a car crash victim because they could not give an appropriate emergency treatment, though, they are responsible for attempting to get help for the victim. This is because they do not have the relevant knowledge and experience. In contrast, a fully trained doctor (with the correct equipment) would be capable of making the correct diagnosis and carrying out appropriate procedures. Failure of a doctor to help at all in such a situation would generally be regarded as negligent and unethical. Though, if a doctor bahlps and makes a mistake that is considered negligent and unethical, there could be egregious repercussions. An untrained person would only be considered to be negligent for failing to act if they did nothing at all to help and is protected by the

"Good Samaritan" laws if they unintentionally caused more damage and possible loss of life.

A business may approach a professional engineer to certify the safety of a project which is not safe. While one engineer may refuse to certify the project on moral grounds, the business may find a less scrupulous engineer who will be prepared to certify the project for a bribe, thus saving the business the expense of redesigning.

Some corporations have tried to burnish their ethical image by creating whistle-blower protections, such as anonymity. In the case of Citi, they call this the "Ethics Hotline",though it is unclear whether firms such as Citi take offences reported to these hotlines seriously or not.

- Separatism

On a theoretical level, there is debate as to whether an ethical code for a profession should be consistent with the requirements of morality governing the public. Separatists argue that professions should be allowed to go beyond such confines when they judge it necessary. This is because they are trained to produce certain outcomes which may take moral precedence over other functions of society. For example, it could be argued that a doctor may lie to a patient about the severity of his or her condition if there is reason to believe that telling the patient would cause so much distress that it would be detrimental to his or her health. This would be a disrespect of the patient's autonomy, as it denies the patient information that could have a great impact on his or her life. This would generally be seen as morally wrong. However, if the end of improving and maintaining health is given a moral priority in society, then it may be justifiable to contravene other moral demands in order to meet this goal. Separatism is based on a relativist conception of morality that there can be different, equally valid, moral codes that apply to different sections of society and differences in codes between societies. If moral universalism is ascribed to, then this would be inconsistent with the view that professions can have a different moral code, as the universalist holds that there is only one valid moral code for all

www.ingramcontent.com/pod-product-compliance
Lightning Source LLC
Chambersburg PA
CBHW022044150726
47990CB00004B/1618